Marketing
Words of Wisdom

By

Steven Howard

Marketing Words of Wisdom

For reprint permission, please contact:
Steven Howard
c/o Caliente Press
1775 E Palm Canyon Drive, #110-198
Palm Springs, CA 92264
USA

Published by:
Caliente Press
1775 E Palm Canyon Drive, #110-198
Palm Springs, CA 92264
USA

Cover Design: Warren White

The following phrases used in this book are trademarked by the author:

If it touches the customer, it's a marketing issue.™

The art of keeping good customers.™

The Art of Keeping Good Customers.™

Table of Contents

Introduction

Over the years I have jotted notes to myself on marketing concepts and various marketing-related ideas, philosophies, and pithy tips. These notes have been spread across several notebooks and scraps of paper.

The main purpose of these has been for use in project work with clients or in my own writing, as I mentally explored how new marketing concepts could be leveraged to improve marketing performance.

About six months ago I started to compile these into *Marketing Words of Wisdom* so that they could be shared with a larger audience. The quotes and phrases in this book are either my own thoughts on marketing or my abridged versions of other people's words. Collectively they form the basis of the marketing and branding advice I give to my own clients.

This book covers four key areas currently impacting the world of marketing today:

Customer Retention

Corporate Image and Branding

Marketing

Marketing As A Business Driver

Written for marketing professionals, non-marketers, business executives, and entrepreneurs, ***Marketing Words of Wisdom*** provides guidance, tips, and directions on the key marketing areas driving future business success.

Enjoy.

Steven Howard
February 2015

Customer Retention

Loyal customers are not an asset just because they buy your products and services. Loyal customers can also help you shape your products, services, communications, distribution channels, target audiences, and markets.

▲▲▲▲▲

Products and services are becoming increasingly commoditized, and the only two ways to distinguish these are your brand and the relationships you have with your good customers (i.e. those who give you repeat business).

▲▲▲▲▲

Focus on customer insights, not data. Marketing must understand customers (Think Like Customers!) and understand how customers think and feel.

▲▲▲▲▲

Customers are always right – even when they are wrong. You job is to correct their misperceptions, errors, and inaccuracies without embarrassing them or making them feel stupid, and the bonds of loyalty thicken and strengthen.

▲▲▲▲▲

In truth, customers are NOT always right – but your job is to do whatever it takes to ensure they leave every encounter with your organization fully satisfied. That is, of course, if you want them to return. If you don't, then don't bother.

▲▲▲▲▲

Inconsistent service delivery is a killer. It eliminates repeat business and slays customer loyalty.

▲▲▲▲▲

Inconsistent customer experience is a killer. It squashes repeat business and sends your loyal customers scurrying away.

▲▲▲▲▲

Customers are most willing to pay for predictability. Some will even pay a significant premium for predictability, assurance, and consistency. When you understand the manner and style of predictability your customers desire or consider important, you are well on the path of sustainable customer retention.

▲▲▲▲▲

Every customer transaction and interaction is a relationship building opportunity. Each transaction either enhances or reduces the relationship in the eyes, minds, hearts, and perceptions of your customers.

▲▲▲▲▲

Customers are human beings, not revenue streams. Treat them as such.

▲▲▲▲▲

If you want your customers and prospects to see you as a unique company – offering unique products and services – you need to see them, and treat them, as *unique individuals* with individual needs, wants, desires, likes, and dislikes.

▲▲▲▲▲

Every customer and every prospect matters. Make sure your actions tell them so.

▲▲▲▲▲

When you know what your customers are buying – and <u>why</u> they are buying – it is easier to satisfy and retain them.

▲▲▲▲▲

Making the creation of customer loyalty your fundamental business strategy driver will enable your organization to better understand your customers and to differentiate (personalize) your products and services based on these insights. Done correctly this produces both rational reasons and emotional connections for customers to return and grants greater wallet share, increased loyalty, positive references, and advocacy for the organization.

▲▲▲▲▲

Customers will respond to service, product and experience problems with their feet (or fingers).....by walking (or clicking) their way to your competitors.

▲▲▲▲▲

The closing of every sale is the beginning (or the continuance) of a relationship with a customer.

▲▲▲▲▲

The customer may not always be right, but there is little success to be found in proving them wrong.

▲ ▲ ▲ ▲ ▲

At every point of customer interface there must be a reaffirmation of the organization's corporate values and behavior in order to strengthen the bonds of customer affinity and loyalty.

▲ ▲ ▲ ▲ ▲

Time spent with customers is rarely wasted.

▲ ▲ ▲ ▲ ▲

The service you are not obliged to give provides the greatest value.

▲ ▲ ▲ ▲ ▲

It is what you do – after you do what you are expected to do – that matters most to customers.

▲ ▲ ▲ ▲ ▲

Truly great companies integrate and embed customer loyalty into their cultures, making this a vital business operation that creates long-term, sustainable business growth and profitability.

▲ ▲ ▲ ▲ ▲

It is less expensive, easier, and more profitable to market new products and services to existing customers than it is to market existing products and services to new customers.

▲ ▲ ▲ ▲ ▲

Professor Peter Drucker is still right: the real purpose of business is to understand how to attract and keep customers.

▲▲▲▲▲

Here's the catch about little things: if you take them for granted, they cease to remain as little things.

To your customers, however, there is no such thing as a little thing!

▲▲▲▲▲

Organizations will continue to lose business unless they learn to tailor their products and services to meet individual needs.

▲▲▲▲▲

Your most dissatisfied customers are your greatest source of learning; but only if you have systems, processes and procedures for listening to them and then putting into action remedies and prevention of repeat occurrence.

▲▲▲▲▲

Teach your staff not to be afraid to ask customers if they are fully satisfied.

Without asking, you will never know your customers' true feelings. By asking, your organization shows you care and that you want these customers to return to do more business with you.

▲▲▲▲▲

Customer Loyalty Categories

Loyalists (or Advocates) – truly loyal customers. Currently use your products and services and would recommend these to friends, colleagues or business prospects. This group is the <u>foundation</u> of future business.

Accessible – customers who like you but may not necessarily recommend you to others. Could be temporary customers pending life-style or segment changes.

Trapped – customers who have reasons for not liking you and would switch if they had the chance. High switching costs or lack of viable options keep them as customers, but it is likely they are high-maintenance customers due to complaints, price negotiations, and time consuming interactions with your staff.

Unloyal – category where lost customers and former customers are most likely to be found. These customers do not like you and are unlikely to stay with you. They could also be trial users, who may migrate to one of the other three categories depending on their experiences with your products, services, and staff.

▲▲▲▲▲

The old rule of marketing: create good products for average people. This no longer works. Today you need to create products, services, and experiences for individual customers.

▲ ▲ ▲ ▲ ▲

To become more profitable, organizations need a customer strategy guided by customer insights and focused on building emotional and rational connections with individual customers.

▲ ▲ ▲ ▲ ▲

Customers determine who they want to have a relationship with. Build your relationship skills to be flexible and adaptable, and applicable to those who <u>want to receive</u> them.

Some customers do not want relationships. Fine....serve them efficiently and effectively and respect their wishes. Do not try to sell them on a relationship! In return, they will appreciate and respect you – and will return to do business with you when their needs arise again.

▲ ▲ ▲ ▲ ▲

Many organizations focus on trying to avoid bad customer experiences and recovering from those that do occur – but only the GREAT ones focus on delivering superior, enhancing, and uplifting customer experiences.

▲ ▲ ▲ ▲ ▲

Customers are more forgiving when an error occurs from an organization that delivers overall superior service than from those whose customer service delivery is ordinary or standard.

Surprisingly this is true even despite the higher expectations of the former based on previous experiences or brand promises. It is much like how you would more readily forgive a friend for a faux pas than you would a mere acquaintance or a stranger.

Familiarity and positive past interactions breed forgiveness.

▲▲▲▲▲

Only two kinds of people should work in any organization:

    1) those who serve customers, and

    2) those who serve those serving customers.

Anyone else is overhead and needs to start serving.

▲▲▲▲▲

Customer loyalty is won by many actions, and lost by as few as one.

▲▲▲▲▲

Customers usually treat you the way you treat them. Treat customers with respect, dignity, and honesty and they will continue to return to do business with you.

▲▲▲▲▲

What customers want most of all is choice and flexibility.

▲ ▲ ▲ ▲ ▲

Your customers want choice. More importantly, they simply want what <u>they</u> want.

▲ ▲ ▲ ▲ ▲

Your entire customer retention strategy should be based on the experiences your customers go through in their interactions with your organization.

▲ ▲ ▲ ▲ ▲

Loyalty programs often leave customers caring more about points and rewards than your brand. This is not a sustainable way to build long-term loyalty for a brand or your business.

▲ ▲ ▲ ▲ ▲

You cannot keep customers unless you earn their fealty. No fealty = no loyalty.

▲ ▲ ▲ ▲ ▲

Customer experience is easily the single most important criterion determining where repeat business is won or lost. Without providing value or appreciated customer experiences, you will not maximize the opportunity to turn trial users into truly loyal customers.

▲ ▲ ▲ ▲ ▲

New customer acquisition is an investment cost.

Profitability is built on customer retention.

▲ ▲ ▲ ▲ ▲

Stupid fees turn away smart customers.

▲ ▲ ▲ ▲ ▲

Customers own the relationship – you cannot manage what you do not own!

(And hence the misnomer of Customer Relationship Management.)

▲ ▲ ▲ ▲ ▲

The Golden Rule of treating customers as you want to be treated is actually a faulty premise. It is far better to treat customers as they want to be treated. Do not assume your customers have the same needs, wants, desires, likes, and dislikes as you (or even each other). Doing so is usually a wrong assumption.

▲ ▲ ▲ ▲ ▲

Selling is the art of converting shoppers into buyers. Marketing is the art of turning prospects and one-time consumers into loyal customers.

▲ ▲ ▲ ▲ ▲

Customers value convenience. What is your strategy for minimizing the effort required to conduct business with you? What is your strategy for making life more convenient for your customers?

▲ ▲ ▲ ▲ ▲

Mystery shoppers tell you what your staff are doing, but not what your customers are feeling and thinking.

▲ ▲ ▲ ▲ ▲

Find an appealing aspect for each customer interaction.

▲ ▲ ▲ ▲ ▲

Smiles result in sales.

▲ ▲ ▲ ▲ ▲

Put the customer relationship before the task at hand.

▲ ▲ ▲ ▲ ▲

Add value at every level of the relationship through every interaction and point of interaction.

▲ ▲ ▲ ▲ ▲

Key question: how does your business make your customers feel?

▲ ▲ ▲ ▲ ▲

Think about the effects you create on your customers, not the functionality of your processes. What effect is the business creating?

▲▲▲▲▲

Don't focus on how customers feel about you; focus on how you make customers feel about themselves!

▲▲▲▲▲

Are your marketing dollars buying customers – or just renting them?

▲▲▲▲▲

The customer may not always be right, but it is your responsibility to ensure that they walk out of your place of business completely satisfied.

▲▲▲▲▲

The secret to Customer Retention Marketing is TLC (think like customers).

▲▲▲▲▲

A person or business is not your customer until the second time they buy. The first time they purchase they are merely a trial user.

▲▲▲▲▲

That's not our policy simply means "we do not care about your personal needs" to a customer.

▲ ▲ ▲ ▲ ▲

Someone in every organization should be responsible for growing customer value.

This role has two key responsibilities:

    a)   preventing customer attrition, and

    b)   growing the value of today's individual customers to a higher value tomorrow.

Both of these roles are measurable. Both can – and should – be rewarded.

▲ ▲ ▲ ▲ ▲

Customers seek reassurance. You need to give them assurances and certainty that they are making the right decision in continuing to do business with you.

▲ ▲ ▲ ▲ ▲

When there is a disconnect between the behavior of the organization and the promises made through marketing communications and marketing, customers will look for alternative solution providers. Failure to prevent such disconnect results in failure to keep good customers.

▲ ▲ ▲ ▲ ▲

Repeat customers are not necessarily loyal customers. Repeat (but non-loyal) customers are more price sensitive and are less likely to recommend you to others.

▲ ▲ ▲ ▲ ▲

Keep former customers from becoming vigilantes, defined as those who spread negative comments about your products, services, staff, brands, and reputation.

▲ ▲ ▲ ▲ ▲

Customers are your only source of revenue. Repeat customers are your key source for sustainable revenues. Products and services do not create revenue – customers do.

▲ ▲ ▲ ▲ ▲

The customer retention 80/20 rule:

20% of customers produce 80% of profits
80% of customers require 80% of costs

▲ ▲ ▲ ▲ ▲

Every good marketer knows it costs less to retain a repeating customer than it does to acquire a new one.

What if you spent just as much time, effort and money to keep good customers as you do to acquire new ones? Wouldn't this double, perhaps even triple, your customer retention ratio?

Wouldn't this lead to a core of brand advocates spreading your key marketing messages and doing your new customer acquisition work for you?

How powerful would this be?

▲ ▲ ▲ ▲ ▲

Most customer acquisition in many ways is just trading customers with your competition. They steal five of your customers and you persuade five of theirs to come to you.

You would be better off keeping your five customers from leaving in the first place.

▲▲▲▲▲

CRM to date has mostly been a sales tracking tool, occasionally used to attempt cross-selling and up-selling.

Only idiots would base a relationship model on what they have sold, or would like to sell to customers. Other than prostitutes, of course!

▲▲▲▲▲

If you want a long-term relationship with a customer, do not negotiate a one-sided deal.

Remember, you are negotiating a relationship, not just a single transaction. If the other side feels cheated or treated unequally, there is little incentive for them to consider having a relationship with you or your organization.

▲▲▲▲▲

Treat your customers with respect and dignity, while delivering consistent quality at an acceptable price, and the vast majority of your customers will stick with you.

However, try to trick and manipulate them into products and services with little true value to them, or treat them like suckers, and you will earn the disrespect, scorn and contempt you receive in turn.

▲▲▲▲▲

Imagine a scenario where it becomes impossible to obtain any new customers.

How would that change what your marketing team does all day? How would that change your marketing plans and budgets?

What would happen if you started acting this way immediately?

▲▲▲▲▲

Corporate Image and Branding

Employees are one of the best ways to communicate your brand's true value to customers. Each employee interaction with a customer either denigrates or builds upon the brand promise.

▲ ▲ ▲ ▲ ▲

The brand value you deliver to customers actually changes their behavior, which in turn delivers value back to your business. This is not an "exchange" of value, but rather the co-creation of enhanced value to both parties.

▲ ▲ ▲ ▲ ▲

The old model of brand building, only via one-way brand monologues is dead. Building great brands comes through deep, rich, emotional connections with passionate customers.

▲ ▲ ▲ ▲ ▲

Don't decide upon a marketing message, determine a positioning platform.

▲ ▲ ▲ ▲ ▲

Corporate slogans may limit reasons for relationship building. Make sure your slogan appeals widely and deeply to all your potential customers and stakeholders.

▲ ▲ ▲ ▲ ▲

At every point of customer interface there must be a reaffirmation of your organization's corporate values and behavior in order to strengthen the bonds and values attached to the corporate brand.

▲ ▲ ▲ ▲ ▲

An uncaring organization cannot have a good corporate image or a stellar corporate reputation.

▲ ▲ ▲ ▲ ▲

Reputation is the single most important marketing asset you have.

▲ ▲ ▲ ▲ ▲

Reputation is a performance bond that connotes an informal contract between your organization and your customers.

▲ ▲ ▲ ▲ ▲

Organizations cannot ask for trust – they must demonstrate that they are trustworthy.

▲ ▲ ▲ ▲ ▲

Branding is the one and only asset that competitors cannot destroy or beat through pricing.

▲ ▲ ▲ ▲ ▲

Three Rules for Good Corporate Branding:

1. You must always look and act unmistakably like you.

2. Your brand must be the star of all communications (not the user and definitely not as the butt of jokes).

3. Brand characteristics must be apparent even to those who do not think of you as a solution for their needs or who currently purchase from others in your product category.

▲▲▲▲▲

There is a myth that brands get built through stellar advertising.

In truth, the exact opposite generally occurs. Brands get built by grassroots adoption and word of mouth referrals, because they live up to their promises.

These promises get communicated and reinforced by advertising, not created by advertising.

▲▲▲▲▲

How important is your brand?

Quite frankly, corporate image brand management is simply about the enduring, profitable growth of your business.

▲▲▲▲▲

Products offer solutions.

Brands help to define the customer's social status and/or to communicate their social status/level of wealth to others.

A watch tells the time. A Rolex watch communicates much more than the time of day.

▲ ▲ ▲ ▲ ▲

When customers get what they expect from a brand, they will stick with it until something more enticing comes along. When customers continually receive <u>more</u> than what they expect from a brand, they will remain <u>more</u> loyal to it.

▲ ▲ ▲ ▲ ▲

A brand comprises three attributes:

1) the brand domain – what customers and others consider the brand offer to be.

2) the brand reputation – what customers and others consider the brand to stand for.

3) the brand affinity – the bond customers and others feel toward the brand.

▲ ▲ ▲ ▲ ▲

Brand deceit is not delivering on the brand promise, especially by customer-facing staff.

▲ ▲ ▲ ▲ ▲

Reputation is earned through corporate behavior. It is also lost through behavior.

Marketing can help build an expected behavior, but actual execution against expectations is what determines your corporate reputation.

▲▲▲▲▲

Your brand image is maintained or tarnished at every customer point of interaction.

Wherever and whenever customers spend time with your organization, your brand image is enhanced, preserved, or blemished.

On the Internet, this takes place with each click. In the physical world this takes place in each face-to-face encounter with your staff, premises, and products.

▲▲▲▲▲

Investors pay up front for the respect garnered through a strong corporate image, in part because respected companies tend to hold their market values longer, even in times of market downturns.

▲▲▲▲▲

A good name, like good will, is won through many acts and actions, and can be lost by just one.

▲▲▲▲▲

To achieve any success, a brand name must be inherently linked to a positive and valued idea in the mind of the prospective customer.

Even a well-known brand name does not have marketing value if there is no linkage to something of positive value in the mind of the customer.

▲▲▲▲▲

A brand can connect emotionally and rationally with customers only if it is perceived as trustworthy, reliable, and able to dependably and consistently meet all customer expectations at each point of interaction.

▲▲▲▲▲

A brand is <u>the source</u> of promises to your customers.

These promises <u>must</u> be delivered upon at each point of interaction for the brand to survive and grow.

▲▲▲▲▲

Competitors can mimic any product, price, marketing campaign or distribution strategy.

Competitors can outspend you on product development, promotions, distribution, and can also beat you up on pricing.

However, the one thing that competitors cannot copy, mimic or beat is a well-defined corporate personality.

▲▲▲▲▲

Marketing

It is not what you communicate; it is what your customers hear.

▲▲▲▲▲

Customers are the heart of every business. Customers pay your bills with their payments.

▲▲▲▲▲

You are unlikely to experience a shortage of products or services you can market.

However, if you do not market properly, a shortage of customers is a predictable outcome.

▲▲▲▲▲

Profitability is not very useful or informative for understanding customer needs.

▲▲▲▲▲

The increasing power of customers – combined with the ever increasing empowerment of customers to use self-service channels when, where, and how they like – increases the importance of touch points, and requires marketing to extend beyond marketing communications into actual business and customer retention strategies.

▲▲▲▲▲

If it touches the customer, it's a marketing issue.™

▲ ▲ ▲ ▲ ▲

Every customer is a unique and individual customer, with individual needs, wants, desires, likes, and dislikes.

▲ ▲ ▲ ▲ ▲

Personalization can happen only at the point of sale (including the virtual point of sale).

▲ ▲ ▲ ▲ ▲

Marketing used to lead customers to the product channel. Now smart marketers let customers do the leading, allowing customers to be in control.

▲ ▲ ▲ ▲ ▲

Sales is a part of Marketing. Ideally the Sales Director and the Head of Customer Service would report to the Marketing Director (in a marketing-driven, customer-centric organization).

▲ ▲ ▲ ▲ ▲

Marketing defines the brand, communicates the value proposition, and generates the sales leads. The sales team closes the deal. Both are responsible for ensuring the consistency of the customer's post-purchase experiences.

▲ ▲ ▲ ▲ ▲

Customers have learned how to filter out traditional marketing communications messages – and with devices such as TiVo, RSS, news delivery apps, and SPAM filters they have increasingly have more tools to do so.

▲ ▲ ▲ ▲ ▲

Marketing results would improve dramatically if organizations paid more attention to their interactions when customers reach out to them, instead of focusing so much on their own interactions when they reach out to customers and prospects.

▲ ▲ ▲ ▲ ▲

Understand the role your products have in people's and customer's lives. Why do they buy your product? How do they use it? When do they use it?

▲ ▲ ▲ ▲ ▲

Internet groups are the new geography of target audiences and target markets.

People are gathering around their interests, through the Internet. The better those interest groups can be identified, and your products / services designed to meet these common needs, the better you can serve and sell them. It is still segmentation, just not based on typical demographics.

▲ ▲ ▲ ▲ ▲

Behavioral change happens by speaking to people's feelings. Emotional persuasion creates long-lasting behavioral change. Emotional appeals are the start of long-term customer relationships.

▲ ▲ ▲ ▲ ▲

The availability and fluidity of information has resulted in unprecedented customer power. From a marketing perspective, we are entering the true age of People Power.

▲▲▲▲▲

The competitive arena today is the customer's experience.

▲▲▲▲▲

Discerning customers want customized solutions. It is really that simple.

▲▲▲▲▲

Marketing is <u>the</u> integrator across all lines of a business, all departments, all divisions.

▲▲▲▲▲

Create – don't compete.

(This is the Blue Ocean strategy boiled down to three words.)

▲▲▲▲▲

Innovate – don't hesitate.

▲▲▲▲▲

Create a uniqueness that appeals to people who will respond to this uniqueness.

▲▲▲▲▲

Price is what you charge.

Value is what you deliver.

Price accordingly.

▲▲▲▲▲

The first rule of marketing: know your market.

The second rule of marketing: understand your customers.

▲▲▲▲▲

Marketing begins with how your customers will interact with your products, services and organization (including indirect links to your organization such as channel partners, co-brand partners, and other marketing intermediaries).

▲▲▲▲▲

Marketing integrity is being true to what your brand represents and consistency in how this is delivered; and has nothing to do with ethics or law abiding integrity.

▲▲▲▲▲

Forget your products. It is your prospects and your customers that matter.

▲▲▲▲▲

Four rules for advertising:

> Engage – ads must be worth watching/reading more than once.

> Brand Build – build memory structures in audiences and readers so they know how your brand looks, acts, and feels.

> Show – the solution you are selling, where/how it is used or consumed, and who buys it.

> Reach – your core target market (customers, prospects and potential influencers on future customers) with spillover to occasional buyers and non-buyers.

▲ ▲ ▲ ▲ ▲

If the customer does not win, no one wins!

▲ ▲ ▲ ▲ ▲

Marketing is not rocket science; it is the science <u>and art</u> of:

- Identifying market opportunities
- Building brands
- Developing new products / services and entering new markets
- Creating customer loyalty and repeat business

▲ ▲ ▲ ▲ ▲

Marketing budgets should not be considered discretionary.

▲ ▲ ▲ ▲ ▲

There is a misplaced focus on marketing metrics today.

The number one thing to measure is your customers' propensity to repeat their business with you.

Secondly, measure how likely are they to bring to you new customers or to refer potential customers, colleagues, and friends to you.

▲ ▲ ▲ ▲ ▲

A competitive advantage is what you do different from and/or better than your competition.

It is the service, product, brand identification, guarantee, or anything else that motivates the customer to give you his or her money because price is no longer the main issue or the deciding point of differentiation.

▲ ▲ ▲ ▲ ▲

An advertising campaign should be timely.

A branding campaign should be timeless.

▲ ▲ ▲ ▲ ▲

Having a marketing strategy is paramount. Tactical execution alone will not develop and grow a sustainable business.

▲ ▲ ▲ ▲ ▲

Product Benefits

Traditional benefits – how the product is engineered.

Functional benefits – the experiences provided to the customer or user.

Emotional benefits – how it makes the buyer, user and customer feel.

Get these product benefits right and the result is increased customer loyalty (behavior) and customer satisfaction (attitude).

▲ ▲ ▲ ▲ ▲

Many companies have reacted to increased globalization by cutting costs and focusing on their bottom lines.

Market leaders are the few who invest in marketing to grow their top lines (revenue, market share, and customer retention).

▲ ▲ ▲ ▲ ▲

Marketing is going to get fun again.

The use of new technologies (Web 2.0 / 3.0, social media and mobility marketing) ratchets up the ability of marketers to engage customers on more personal, relevant, and timely levels.

▲ ▲ ▲ ▲ ▲

Success in the Web 2.0 world (and beyond) for many brands will be determined by their ability to be found by customers, and by the ease in ability for people to recommend / refer brands to their friends and social networking groups.

▲ ▲ ▲ ▲ ▲

Self-service implementations can help drive customer expectations to a level where they expect (and appreciate) more availability of information and the freedom to choose when and how they initiate customer service.

But, self-service needs to be based on what your customers need, not only on lowering your delivery costs.

▲ ▲ ▲ ▲ ▲

Marketing is basically nothing more than matching people to the things they need and then to the things they desire (ala Maslow's Hierarchy of Needs).

This is why the most effective marketing is based on knowledge of human nature and what motivates people individually and collectively. Marketing needs to help people achieve the satisfaction of their desires.

▲ ▲ ▲ ▲ ▲

If you try to grow your business in areas where you do not have either a significant compelling advantage or differentiation, you will stir up a great number of opportunities for your competitors to win based on their significant compelling advantages or differentiation.

▲ ▲ ▲ ▲ ▲

Marketing is not a method used to sell what you produce or provide.

Marketing is the art of gaining new customers through creating superb customer value combined with *the art of keeping good customers.*™

▲▲▲▲▲

Many people have forgotten what business is all about. They think it is about systems, processes, cost containment, and bottom line profits. These, however, are the mere consequences of being in business and managing your business.

The purpose of a business is to provide something that customers want at a cost (in terms of money, time, and convenience) that they are willing and prepared to pay.

It is with the customer that all business decisions should start and end.

Everything else is detail.

▲▲▲▲▲

Marketing is core to value adding. Great marketing adds to your core value proposition.

Anything less than great marketing simply adds cost to your equation.

▲▲▲▲▲

Mass media made marketing too easy for the lazy and those with big budgets.

My, how times have changed!

▲ ▲ ▲ ▲ ▲

Providing too many choices and options to customers can be confusing.

The role of choice is not to give customers too many options, but to provide you with more customers who match their needs with the range you provide.

It is all about how you communicate.

▲ ▲ ▲ ▲ ▲

Value and quality are relative measures. The judgment criteria and evaluation of these rests with your customers – and no one else!

▲ ▲ ▲ ▲ ▲

Every individual customer is really two people: the person they are (or believe themselves to be) and the person they want to be (or imagine themselves becoming).

The role of marketing is to associate a product or service with one or both of these personal visions.

▲ ▲ ▲ ▲ ▲

Products and services are relative perceptions – relative to the customer's situation and perceptions at the time and place of the purchase decision process.

▲▲▲▲▲

Old school marketing is about getting customers to do what you want them to do.

Web marketing is about helping customers do the things they want to do conveniently.

▲▲▲▲▲

You can (and should) build a reputation in everything you do.

If people trust you, then you can retain their attention and receive permission to continue communicating with them.

This will become exceedingly valuable in a world of customers who get more skeptical by the day and who have easier and greater access to both information and the offers from your competitors.

▲▲▲▲▲

The best corporate trait for today is agility.

Agility results from being able, as an organization, to adjust to changing needs through being aware of changes in the operating and marketing environment.

Agility demands flexibility of resources. Agility demands flexibility of thinking. Agility requires flexibility in applying policies, processes and procedures.

▲▲▲▲▲

CEX = Customer Experience.

Which means: CEX sells!

▲▲▲▲▲

You market to your customers. You sell to everyone else.

▲▲▲▲▲

Today, customers have great influence through word of mouth and mouse.

▲▲▲▲▲

Warning: engaging in communications with customers, and then ignoring the feedback received, is actually worse than simply not engaging customers in the first place.

Raising customer expectations through dialogue and interaction, only to show that the organization is not truly listening and reacting, leads to a greater level of disappointment than if you had merely not engaged or pretended to listen at all.

▲▲▲▲▲

To be effective at marketing, you must understand that everyone has a different perspective about the world (and their significant piece of it).

Successful marketers use this understanding as their guide on how to effectively communicate with their target audiences.

▲▲▲▲▲

Social media is a totally different marketplace and communication channel, which complements (and sometime replaces) traditional markets and communication channels.

If you are not getting involved in this interactive market and communication channel, you risk becoming less relevant every day as your prospects and customers segue to places where your brand is non-existent and you have no voice or influence.

▲ ▲ ▲ ▲ ▲

Information is of real value to consumers. Easy access to information is highly valued. Helping customers translate information into knowledge is even more highly valued.

If you have information, deliver it in as many easy accessible channels as feasible. And then help customers understand and apply this information.

Engage and entice your prospects and customers through – and with – your relevant information.

▲ ▲ ▲ ▲ ▲

Word of mouth (and mouse) is becoming one of the most powerful forms of communication in B2B marketing.

It has longed ranked in the top five list of powerful communications for B2C marketing.

▲ ▲ ▲ ▲ ▲

Ask: are you selling nails or empowering someone to build a bird house?

▲ ▲ ▲ ▲ ▲

People always comment that you have only one chance to make a good first impression.

While true, the fact is also that you have only one chance to make a good last (and lasting) impression.

The last impression made can be far more important.

For example, a flight leaves on time, arrives early, and the service on board was impeccable. But the customer's luggage doesn't arrive on the carousel belt.

Which aspect of the journey are they most likely to remember.....and to tell others?

▲ ▲ ▲ ▲ ▲

The best way to sell is to make it convenient to buy from you.

▲ ▲ ▲ ▲ ▲

Marketing has three key roles:

1) Build the brand.
2) Deliver great experiences that meet customer expectations.
3) Create loyal customers who repeatedly purchase and who constantly recommend the brand.

▲ ▲ ▲ ▲ ▲

A <u>great</u> marketing person will do everything in their power to prevent the creation or implementation of sales, distribution, pricing and promotional strategies that are not in the long-term best interest of the brand.

A sales person will naturally sell to anyone, via any channel, at any price they can obtain.

For this very reason, it is often not a good idea to move someone from sales into marketing and brand management.

It is also why many smart entrepreneurs, with their incessant focus on cash flows and burn rates, hire professional marketing heads and leave the marketing and sales strategies to them if they want to build a sustainable, long-term business with a sustainable brand image.

▲▲▲▲▲

If your customers adopt new technologies and new communication channels faster than you do, your organization risks becoming irrelevant and unnoticeable to them.

▲▲▲▲▲

Do want you promise. Customers and prospects have long memories.

▲▲▲▲▲

Your customers are increasingly faster and more informed.

What are you doing to keep up with them?

▲ ▲ ▲ ▲ ▲

A marketing segment is simply a group of customers who want the same thing or who have very similar needs.

Demographic segmentation is merely a start to good segmentation.

Having a group of customers who share a gender, age range, or who live within flying distance of one another does not constitute a marketing segment.

Think of this initial grouping as a cluster.

Now dig deeper to find commonality of needs, purposes, buying motivations, and lifestyles. Then you will have a true, marketable segment.

▲ ▲ ▲ ▲ ▲

A target segmentation of few customers who are more loyal and who buy more frequently is usually better than a broader based target audience.....unless you have the knowledge and means to convert the broader base into more loyal and frequent purchasers.

▲ ▲ ▲ ▲ ▲

Customers have become better informed than ever before, with the result that some traditional communications methods for marketing and advertising simply no longer work as well as in the past.

You need to incorporate better and more relevant methods of communicating with customers if you want them to stick around.

▲ ▲ ▲ ▲ ▲

"Pink & Shrink" does not equal marketing to women!

▲ ▲ ▲ ▲ ▲

People are tiring of one-way, mass advertising messages in all their forms.

The constant bombardment of advertising messages with little individual relevance has resulted in an evolutionary human trait – the ability to tune out advertising messages almost at will.

▲ ▲ ▲ ▲ ▲

People now distrust companies and products they cannot research on the Internet.

A sign of the times: if a company, brand, or product is not researchable in the virtual world, it is distrusted in the real world.

▲ ▲ ▲ ▲ ▲

As knowledge proliferates and becomes more accessible, products will continue to become more commoditized in the minds of customers and prospects.

As products and services become increasingly commoditized and undifferentiated, the two best ways to distinguish your product and service offers are through your brand and the relationships you build with your customers.

▲ ▲ ▲ ▲ ▲

Segment by communities. A community is a gathering of people (physically and/or virtually) with shared interests, insights, or perspectives.

The Internet provides communities with a platform and the technology to easily interact with one another, for the sharing, distribution, or creation of content.

Communities (and thus market segments) are all about content:

- the exchange of content
- generation of content
- sharing of content
- co-generation of content
- finding relevant content
- evaluating content

▲ ▲ ▲ ▲ ▲

To work effectively, viral marketing must become an active conversation:

- Between the organization and its customers / stakeholders.
- Between people within the community.
- Between the community and the outside world (i.e. other communities).

You cannot control viral marketing. You may be able to jump start it, but once it gets going it will have a life all its own.

▲ ▲ ▲ ▲ ▲

It is therefore little wonder that the connective, social-based technologies and networks of the Internet are particularly appealing to women.

Hence, effective marketing to women today requires making use of these social-based technologies and networks.

▲ ▲ ▲ ▲ ▲

Look at all these recent trends:

EMM – Enterprise Marketing Management
CEM – Customer Experience Management
CRM – Customer Relationship Management

Not only is the focus wrongly placed on management functions, but at the end of the day true success is really all about the basics of marketing and understanding that *if it touches the customer, it's a marketing issue.*™

▲ ▲ ▲ ▲ ▲

The new school of customer acquisition:

Old School	New School
Static	Fluid
One-dimensional	Multi-dimensional
Generic promotion	Personalized offers
Customer acquisition	Customer lifecycle
Cost of acquisition	Customer Lifetime Value

▲ ▲ ▲ ▲ ▲

Change your USP (unique selling proposition) to a UBR (unique buying reason).

The more unique the reason for why people <u>want</u> to buy your products and services, the stronger will be your marketing proposition.

▲▲▲▲▲

For customers who interact with your organization strictly (or mostly) through your web site, you are your web site.

This is the key reason why your corporate web site should be the responsibility of your marketing department, not your IT team.

After all, if your web site is touching your customers, it's a marketing issue!

▲▲▲▲▲

Marketing As A Business Driver

Everyone is an individual customer and deserves to be treated with respect, courtesy and professionalism.

▲▲▲▲▲

As the era of individualized products and personalization continues, customers will increasingly want to participate in the design (and delivery options) of the products and services they use.

▲▲▲▲▲

Front line customer service drives bottom line profitability.

▲▲▲▲▲

Great companies are built on ideals, not deals.

▲▲▲▲▲

The High Road is the only road to a sustainable future.

▲▲▲▲▲

True sustainable business success results from ideas and implementation, not deals and financial manipulation.

▲▲▲▲▲

Growth comes from investing in people resources, not cutting head count in the hopes of reaching new levels of cost effectiveness.

▲ ▲ ▲ ▲ ▲

Increasing customer value long term is far more important than increasing shareholder returns short term.

▲ ▲ ▲ ▲ ▲

If you want to trim the fat, go to the gym, not to the HR department.

▲ ▲ ▲ ▲ ▲

The customer experience is an integral part of the loyalty equation.

▲ ▲ ▲ ▲ ▲

Successful Internet marketing is not about getting customers to do what you want them to, but actually about helping customers to do what they want.

▲ ▲ ▲ ▲ ▲

The old way of marketing: find, flog, forget.

No wonder customers are jaded recipients of marketing messages.

▲ ▲ ▲ ▲ ▲

A key question: do you try to make things easy for your customers?

▲ ▲ ▲ ▲ ▲

Eliminate stupid fees. Now.

I once read where a company charged new customers an "account activation fee."

Why?

This sort of fee is only going to irritate and aggravate prospects and customers.

You might as well call this an "account aggravation fee," as in *it is so aggravating to have to open up new accounts for new customers.*

▲ ▲ ▲ ▲ ▲

Customers request service. You provide it. No longer end of story.

Instead, start of a relationship.

▲ ▲ ▲ ▲ ▲

Provide customers with something of value and they will pay for it.

▲ ▲ ▲ ▲ ▲

Once you discount your prices, it can take up to <u>seven years</u> before customer perceptions of "normal pricing" returns.

▲ ▲ ▲ ▲ ▲

In order to change a customer's behavior, you need to understand what <u>drives</u> the behavior.

I call this TLC – Thinking Like Customers.

▲ ▲ ▲ ▲ ▲

The difference between the ordinary and the extraordinary is the EXTRA.

▲ ▲ ▲ ▲ ▲

People act the way they are treated.

Treat them like thieves and they will try to cheat you and steal from you.

Treat them with trust and respect and they will be honest in their dealings with you.

▲ ▲ ▲ ▲ ▲

Focus on results, not goals.

Goals are arbitrary benchmarks used to justify budgets.

Results tell you what is happening in the real world (and sometimes why).

▲ ▲ ▲ ▲ ▲

Knowing your strengths and the weaknesses of your competition, you can plan an appropriate marketing strategy.

Knowing your weaknesses and the strengths of your competitors, you can execute that strategy.

▲ ▲ ▲ ▲ ▲

Marketing is centered on creating solutions for customers.

▲ ▲ ▲ ▲ ▲

Regrets and buyer's remorse from sacrificed quality remains with the customer long after the pleasure of a low price has dissipated.

▲ ▲ ▲ ▲ ▲

The central point of contact for the customer with your organization is the central point of control of the customer experience.

This is where your top performers should be placed.

▲ ▲ ▲ ▲ ▲

Ad likeability is a strong predictor of success (in terms of communicating your message).

This is the reason most political advertising does not work – neither the ads nor the politicians are likeable.

Likeability equals empathy, relevance and familiarity; it does not equal entertainment, confusing messages, or negative appeals.

▲ ▲ ▲ ▲ ▲

Marketing success is all about real quality, delivered!

▲ ▲ ▲ ▲ ▲

Sales is merely problem solving; make that customer problem solving.

▲ ▲ ▲ ▲ ▲

Some sales are bad for the long-term interest of the business.

These are the ones that bring you wrong customers and which spread your customer servicing resources too thin. These simply end up costing you money.

These are the ones that start to erode the edges of your finely crafted positioning strategy. These start to tell people that perhaps you no longer are the brand they thought you were.

These are the ones that lead to dissatisfied customers who then speak ill of your organization and its people, products, services and brands. They end up driving prospective customers away from your door (or home page).

These are the ones that capture wrong customer segments that are anathema to your core customer base. These end up losing you the long-term loyal customers that have been the foundation of previous growth and success.

▲ ▲ ▲ ▲ ▲

There is a strong association between likeability and correct brand recall.

That's why product spokespeople and celebrity endorsers need to be likeable <u>to your target audience.</u>

▲ ▲ ▲ ▲ ▲

Rational marketing ignores half a customer's brain.

Customers buy for both rational and emotional reasons. Persuade by reason, motivate through emotion.

This is the Yin and Yang of marketing.

▲ ▲ ▲ ▲ ▲

Not revealing mistakes and identifying how to fix these means those mistakes <u>will be repeated</u>.

▲ ▲ ▲ ▲ ▲

What feelings do you want your customers to have or experience? Why?

▲ ▲ ▲ ▲ ▲

Organizing around functionality is okay, if the whole organization is customer centric.

Otherwise, you need to organize around customer segments <u>or customer centers of excellent experiences</u>!

▲ ▲ ▲ ▲ ▲

You can create a team in a week, but a culture gradually comes into being.

▲ ▲ ▲ ▲ ▲

Envision the future and you can shape it as you move into it.

▲ ▲ ▲ ▲ ▲

Best titles to have:
> Managing Director – Customer Loyalty
> Customer Loyalty Development Director
> Vice President, Customer Loyalty
> Vice President, Customer Retention

New titles to consider:
> CEO: Customer Executive Officer
> CCMO: Chief Customer Marketing Officer (provides relevant marketing information to customers and prospects)
> CIO: Customer Information Officer (provides information relevant to customers)
> CEX: Customer Experience Officer

▲ ▲ ▲ ▲ ▲

A great marketer understands human behavior.

▲ ▲ ▲ ▲ ▲

Technology should be used to enable efficient service. However, there is always a need to provide a personal touch, even when providing self-service options.

▲ ▲ ▲ ▲ ▲

Processes and Procedures are the two best hiding places for people without the wisdom, wit, or passion to do their jobs properly.

▲▲▲▲▲

Value for customers equates to benefits received for burdens (time, money, inconvenience, etc.) endured.

The stronger your benefit-to-burden ratio, the stronger is your offer and your competitive positioning.

▲▲▲▲▲

Value evokes a much wider concept than price or price-to-benefits.

Price is an important component of value perception, but only one component.

Value is the total experience of the customer – set against the burdens (time, money, inconvenience, etc.) required to obtain the experience – while price is simply price.

▲▲▲▲▲

The wide availability and fluidity of information has democratized the world of business and created customers who enjoy and utilize unprecedented knowledge and power.

▲▲▲▲▲

Companies sell using one currency – price.

Customers buy using at least two currencies – price and time.

Sometimes they use a third currency – brand affinity.

Or a fourth – convenience.

Companies tend to be one-dimensional in their selling strategies.

Customers tend to be multi-dimensional in their buying behaviors.

Smart marketers recognize and understand this dichotomy.

▲ ▲ ▲ ▲ ▲

A new marketing equation:

> Product Benefits + Service + Price + Convenience = Baseline Value to Customer

> Culture + People + Policies = Organizational Value (to customers)

> Baseline Value to Customer + Organizational Value = Brand Value (to customers)

▲ ▲ ▲ ▲ ▲

An attitude of *the customer is always right* belittles the importance of your employees.

However, an attitude of *the organi￭ation is a￭wa￭ right* cheapens your customers, insults their dignity, and paves the way for numerous problems.

▲ ▲ ▲ ▲ ▲

Here is why accountants should stay out of marketing — accountancy rules allow a company to count the value of a brand as an asset on its balance sheet only if it buys the brand from another company — but not if it creates the brand itself!

How illogical is that?

▲ ▲ ▲ ▲ ▲

The product promotion cycle rarely matches the customer buying cycle, except for seasonal activities and items.

When a bank pushes credit cards one month and mutual funds the next, this "hit and miss" approach delivers less than optimum results.

▲ ▲ ▲ ▲ ▲

(Marketing + Advertising) multiplied by Customer Engagement = Success

▲ ▲ ▲ ▲ ▲

The front line produces the bottom line.

▲ ▲ ▲ ▲ ▲

Customers simply want to deal with organizations that will listen to them, understand their problems, and related their needs.

When responding, it is more important to SHOW that you care through actions rather than trying to convince them through hollow words or marketing messages that you care.

▲▲▲▲▲

Breakthroughs and innovation come from breaking with the past, stepping away from normal patterns, and refusing to be bound by habits.

▲▲▲▲▲

Policies, rules, and regulations prevent human judgment and creativity. How tightly do you want to bind your staff......the knowledge workers in your business?

▲▲▲▲▲

The **seven most expensive words** for an organization: We have always done it this way!

▲▲▲▲▲

Marketing is the common thread that crosses all levels of the organization, all departments, all functions, and all geographies.

▲▲▲▲▲

The service-dominated economies are transforming into experience-oriented economies where tangible products and product functionality are becoming less important drivers of purchase decisions.

▲▲▲▲▲

We have moved from an era of mass media predominance to an era of meaningful media.

Marketing executions should no longer be campaign driven, but relevance driven.

In today's new media world, relevance is often defined by the ability to forward or share received marketing messages, or the ability to interact with the company or brand sending the marketing message.

▲▲▲▲▲

Everyone reports to someone, and thus everyone has customers.

Whether you report to a boss, supervisor, director, colleagues, voters, or shareholders – these are your customers.

Personal success is gleaned through consistently doing your best to serve the interests of your customers.

▲▲▲▲▲

Criticisms and complaints should always flow up in an organization to a level where they can become a catalyst for change.

Praise should always flow down through an organization to a level where it will have the most positive effect.

Note: if praise or criticisms flow in the opposite direction as described here, the results are generally harmful for both the organization and its people.

▲ ▲ ▲ ▲ ▲

Customers today are increasingly vocal, with their voices and words traveling via an increasing array of social media channels.

Whether you like it or not, they <u>will</u> be talking about you.

Of course, the only thing worse would be if they <u>did not</u> talk about you!

▲ ▲ ▲ ▲ ▲

Organizations have three primary constituencies: customers, employees, and shareholders.

In order to create sustainable value for any one of these, you must also do likewise for the other two.

Too great a focus or concentration on the needs of one of these constituencies, at the expense of the other two, will ultimately result in damage to both the organization and negate the benefits being provided to the third.

▲ ▲ ▲ ▲ ▲

Implementing best practices from someone else is basically an attempt to replicate their past or current successes.

A better methodology is to innovate your way to success by <u>designing your successes</u> of tomorrow.

▲ ▲ ▲ ▲ ▲

The best Chief Marketing Officer any organization can have is a CEO who <u>believes</u> in the power of marketing.

▲ ▲ ▲ ▲ ▲

About the Author

Steven Howard
Author, Marketing and Branding Strategist

Steven Howard is a leading marketing strategist, positioning specialist, consultant, and author whose 35-year marketing and sales career in Asia, Australia and the USA has covered a wide variety of fields, ranging from consumer electronics to publishing and from a national airline to personal financial products.

Founder of **Howard Marketing Services**, he consults on a regular basis to companies in the financial services, education, industrial products, consumer products, restaurants, petroleum, publishing and hospitality fields and serves as a Non-Executive Director in both the profit and non-profit sectors.

He is the author of eight other books:

> ***Corporate Image Management:*** □□ar□eting □iscip□he
>
> ***Powerful Marketing Minutes:*** □□□a□ to □eve□p □ar□et □ea□ership
>
> ***MORE Powerful Marketing Minutes:*** □□□ew □a□ to □eve□p □ar□et □ea□ership
>
> ***Asian Words of Wisdom***
>
> ***Asian Words of Knowledge***

Essential Asian Words of Wisdom

Pillars of Growth: *⬚rategies for ⬚ea⬚ing ⬚ustaina⬚⬚e ⬚rowth*
(co-author with three others)

Motivation Plus Marketing Equals Money
(co-author with four others)

He also writes the ⬚on⬚a⬚⬚orning ⬚ar⬚eting ⬚emo blog, ⬚he ⬚teven ⬚owar⬚⬚ar⬚eting ⬚og and the ⬚eeping ⬚bo⬚⬚ustomers blog.

Contact Details
1775 E Palm Canyon Drive, #110-198
Palm Springs, CA 92264
USA

Skype: stevenbhoward
Email: steven@howard-marketing.com
Twitter: @stevenbhoward
Web site: www.howard-marketing.com

www.ingramcontent.com/pod-product-compliance
Lightning Source LLC
Chambersburg PA
CBHW070819210326
41520CB00011B/2018